CW00821779

The Youtube Success Formula: The Blueprint For Growth

Alex Brightman

Published by Bright publication, 2023.

While every precaution has been taken in the preparation of this book, the publisher assumes no responsibility for errors or omissions, or for damages resulting from the use of the information contained herein.

THE YOUTUBE SUCCESS FORMULA: THE BLUEPRINT FOR GROWTH

First edition. May 18, 2023.

Copyright © 2023 Alex Brightman.

ISBN: 979-8223288398

Written by Alex Brightman.

Also by Alex Brightman

Blogging for Profit: The Ultimate Guide to Making Money
Online
Enlightened Minds: Words of Wisdom from the Greatest
Thinkers
Affiliate Marketing: The Ultimate Guide to Building a
Profitable Online Business
The Youtube Success Formula: The Blueprint For Growth

Table of Contents

__Shree Ganeshay namah__

Dedication

This book is dedicated to all the aspiring YouTubers who have a burning passion, unwavering determination, and an insatiable thirst for success on the YouTube platform. May your creative spirit soar, your channel thrive, and your dreams become a reality.

Preface:

Welcome to "YouTube Success Formula: The Blueprint for Growth." I am thrilled to have you here as we embark on a journey that will transform your YouTube channel and open doors to unlimited possibilities. Whether you're an aspiring creator seeking guidance or an experienced YouTuber looking to take your channel to new heights, this book is designed to equip you with the knowledge, strategies, and inspiration needed to achieve extraordinary success on the world's most influential video-sharing platform.

The power of YouTube is undeniable. It has revolutionised the way we consume content, connect with others, and share our passions with the world. Every day, millions of people log on to YouTube, searching for entertainment, education, inspiration, and more. As a YouTube creator, you have the incredible opportunity to be a part of this global phenomenon, to leave your mark, and to make a difference.

However, building a successful YouTube channel is not without its challenges. It requires dedication, creativity, perseverance, and a deep understanding of the platform's intricacies. It's not just about uploading videos; it's about crafting engaging content, building a loyal community, and navigating the ever-evolving landscape of online video.

I have been fortunate enough to witness the transformative power of YouTube firsthand. As a creator myself, I have experienced the highs and lows, the triumphs and setbacks that come with building and growing a YouTube channel. I have learned valuable lessons along the way, and it is my sincere desire to share these insights with you.

This book is the culmination of years of experience, research, and collaboration with successful creators and industry experts. It is a comprehensive guide that will walk you through the essential elements of YouTube success, providing you with a step-by-step blueprint to follow as you embark on your own journey to greatness.

Throughout these pages, you will discover practical strategies for every stage of your YouTube career. From finding your niche and creating compelling content to optimising your videos for search and engaging with your audience, each chapter is packed with actionable advice, real-world examples, and valuable insights that will propel your channel forward.

But this book is not just about techniques and tactics. It is also about mindset and passion. It is about nurturing your creativity, embracing your unique voice, and staying true to yourself amidst the noise of the online world. It is about understanding that success on YouTube goes beyond numbers and metrics; it is about making a genuine connection with your viewers and leaving a lasting impact.

I want you to know that success on YouTube is within your reach. No matter where you are in your journey, whether you're just starting out or feeling stuck, this book will provide you with the guidance and inspiration you need to overcome obstacles and achieve your goals. It is my hope that by the time you finish reading this book, you will feel empowered, equipped, and excited to take your channel to new heights.

I encourage you to approach this book with an open mind and a willingness to take action. Each chapter is designed to be a stepping stone, building upon the previous one to create a solid foundation for your YouTube success. Take the time to reflect on the concepts, apply the strategies to your own channel, and adapt them to your unique style and audience.

I also want to emphasise that your journey on YouTube is unique to you. While this book provides valuable guidance, it is important to remember that there is no one-size-fits-all formula for success. Your path may differ from others, and that's okay. Embrace your individuality, embrace experimentation, and always stay true to your vision.

As we embark on this journey together, I want to express my deepest gratitude for choosing "YouTube Success Formula: The Blueprint for Growth" as your guide. I am honoured to be a part of your YouTube adventure, and I am excited to witness your growth and achievements.

So, let's dive in, my fellow creator. Let's uncover the secrets, unlock the potential, and write our own success stories on YouTube. The possibilities are endless, and the world is waiting to hear your voice.

Wishing you an incredible and fulfilling journey to YouTube success.

Sincerely,

Alex Brightman

Part-1

The youtube success formula.

Chapter 1:
Introduction

Welcome to the exciting world of YouTube! In this chapter, we'll embark on a journey to explore the phenomenon of YouTube success and its profound impact in the digital age. This book aims to equip you with valuable insights, practical tips, and inspiring stories that will help you navigate the intricacies of building a successful YouTube channel.

The Power of YouTube

YouTube has revolutionised the way we consume media, transforming the internet into a global stage where anyone can showcase their talents, share their passions, and connect with a vast audience. With over 2 billion logged-in monthly users and more than 500 hours of video uploaded every minute, YouTube has become a cultural powerhouse that has redefined the concept of entertainment and communication.

YouTube's influence goes far beyond its sheer numbers. It has given rise to a new breed of content creators, ordinary individuals who have harnessed the platform's potential to reach millions, build communities, and even create lucrative careers. The democratisation of content creation has shattered traditional barriers, allowing for diverse voices, perspectives, and stories to find an audience like never before.

Through the personal experiences and success stories shared in this book, you'll witness the incredible journeys of individuals who started with a camera and a dream, and through their passion, dedication, and strategic approach, achieved remarkable success on YouTube. From makeup gurus and gamers to educational channels and vloggers, these creators have not only amassed millions of subscribers but have also had a profound impact on their viewers' lives.

The Power of Personal Stories

To truly understand the power of YouTube, it's important to hear the stories of those who have experienced its transformative effects firsthand. In this chapter, we'll delve into a few captivating tales that exemplify the potential YouTube holds for creators.

Consider the story of Sarah, a young aspiring musician who started uploading cover songs to YouTube in the confines of her bedroom. Her soulful renditions caught the attention of music lovers worldwide, and she soon found herself with a devoted following eagerly awaiting her next release. Through YouTube, Sarah not only honed her skills but also caught the attention of record labels, leading to a recording contract and the opportunity to share her talent with a global audience.

Then there's Michael, a tech enthusiast who was passionate about sharing his knowledge of gadgets and new technologies. Armed with a camera and an infectious enthusiasm, he began uploading detailed product reviews and tutorials on YouTube. His informative videos struck a chord with viewers, and soon he became a trusted source of information for tech enthusiasts around the world. His success on YouTube opened doors to partnerships with major tech companies, who recognized his influence and sought his expertise.

THE YOUTUBE SUCCESS FORMULA: THE BLUEPRINT FOR GROWTH

These stories are just a glimpse into the vast potential of YouTube. They showcase how a passion combined with strategic content creation and audience engagement can lead to incredible opportunities. But the path to success on YouTube is not without its challenges, and that's precisely why this book exists.

As we delve deeper into the subsequent chapters, we will explore essential strategies for finding your niche, creating compelling content, optimising your videos for search, building a thriving community, and monetizing your channel effectively. We will also address common obstacles and provide guidance on overcoming them, as well as offer a glimpse into the future of YouTube.

So, whether you're an aspiring creator seeking to launch your own YouTube channel or an existing creator looking to take your channel to the next level, this book is your roadmap to YouTube success. Get ready to unlock your creative potential, captivate an audience, and embark on an exhilarating journey in the captivating world of YouTube.

Chapter 2:
The Rise of YouTube

In this chapter, we'll take a fascinating journey through the history and evolution of YouTube, from its humble beginnings to becoming the global sensation it is today. We'll explore how this platform has grown in popularity and discuss the significant milestones and key players who have shaped its remarkable trajectory.

The Birth of YouTube

YouTube was founded by three former PayPal employees—Chad Hurley, Steve Chen, and Jawed Karim—in February 2005. The idea for YouTube emerged from their shared frustration with the limited options for easily sharing and uploading videos online. They set out to create a platform that would democratise video content, making it accessible to anyone with an internet connection.

Early Days and Explosive Growth

YouTube launched to the public in November 2005, and its impact was immediate. Users were quick to embrace the platform's user-friendly interface, intuitive video uploading process, and the ability to easily embed videos on other websites. The viral potential of YouTube became evident as users started sharing and promoting their videos across social media and other online platforms.

By 2006, YouTube had already established itself as the go-to platform for video content, surpassing 100 million video views per day. This impressive growth attracted the attention of major media outlets and content creators, who recognized the platform's enormous reach and potential for engaging audiences.

Google Acquisition and Global Expansion

Recognizing the value of YouTube, Google acquired the platform in November 2006 for a staggering $1.65 billion. This acquisition provided YouTube with the resources and infrastructure necessary for even greater expansion. With Google's backing, YouTube was able to invest in servers, bandwidth, and content partnerships to accommodate its growing user base.

YouTube's popularity soared to new heights as it expanded internationally, making the platform available in multiple languages and regions. This global reach allowed creators from all corners of the world to share their unique stories, culture, and talents with a worldwide audience.

The Rise of Online Video Culture

YouTube not only revolutionised the way we consume video content but also played a significant role in shaping online video culture. It provided a platform for creative expression, enabling individuals to share their talents, opinions, and perspectives on a global scale. Memes, viral challenges, and user-generated content became synonymous with YouTube, fostering a sense of community and shared experiences among viewers.

The Emergence of Key Players

Throughout its journey, YouTube has been instrumental in propelling countless individuals to stardom and establishing influential channels. Early adopters like Smosh, Lonelygirl15, and Fred gained massive followings and demonstrated the power of YouTube as a launching pad for careers in entertainment. As the platform matured, creators such as PewDiePie, Jenna Marbles, and Dude Perfect amassed millions of subscribers, becoming household names in the digital realm.

YouTube has also witnessed the emergence of diverse genres and content niches. Beauty gurus, gamers, educational channels, comedy skits, and music covers are just a few examples of the wide range of content that thrives on the platform. Each niche has its own community and dedicated creators who have found success by catering to specific audience interests.

Monetization and Partnerships

As YouTube grew, it introduced various monetization opportunities for creators. The YouTube Partner Program, launched in 2007, allowed creators to earn revenue from ads displayed on their videos. This opened the door for aspiring creators to turn their passion into a full-fledged career. Over

THE YOUTUBE SUCCESS FORMULA: THE BLUEPRINT
FOR GROWTH

the years, YouTube expanded its monetization options, including channel memberships, merchandise shelves, Super Chat, and YouTube Premium subscriptions.

Simultaneously, brands and advertisers recognized the vast reach and influence of YouTube creators, leading to fruitful partnerships and sponsorship opportunities. Influencer marketing became a thriving industry, with brands collaborating with popular creators to promote their products and services to a highly engaged audience.

In Conclusion

YouTube's rise has been nothing short of extraordinary. What started as a platform for sharing homemade videos has evolved into a global phenomenon, transforming the entertainment landscape and empowering millions of creators worldwide. Its growth, coupled with the diverse content it hosts and the countless success stories it has spawned, showcases the immense power and impact of YouTube in the digital age.

In the subsequent chapters, we'll delve deeper into the strategies and insights necessary for achieving success on YouTube. We'll explore how to find your niche, create compelling content, optimise your videos, engage with your audience, and monetize your channel effectively. The journey to YouTube success awaits, so let's dive in and unlock the potential that this remarkable platform has to offer.

Chapter 3:
Understanding the YouTube Ecosystem

In this chapter, we'll explore the intricacies of the YouTube ecosystem, breaking down its different components and discussing the roles of creators, viewers, advertisers, and YouTube itself. We'll also introduce key terms and concepts that are essential for achieving success on YouTube, all explained in simple language to ensure a clear understanding.

The YouTube ecosystem consists of various interconnected components that work together to create a thriving platform for video content. Let's examine each component:

Creators: Creators are individuals or groups who produce and upload videos to their YouTube channels. They are the driving force behind the content on YouTube and play a vital role in attracting and engaging viewers.

Viewers: Viewers are the audience members who watch videos on YouTube. They are essential to the success of creators as their views, likes, comments, and shares contribute to a video's popularity and visibility.

Advertisers: Advertisers are businesses and brands that promote their products or services on YouTube. They utilise the platform's advertising features to reach a wide audience and engage with viewers.

THE YOUTUBE SUCCESS FORMULA: THE BLUEPRINT FOR GROWTH

YouTube: YouTube, as the platform itself, serves as the intermediary between creators, viewers, and advertisers. It provides the infrastructure, technology, and tools necessary for content creation, distribution, and monetization.

Roles and Interactions within the YouTube Ecosystem

Now that we understand the different components, let's explore the roles and interactions within the YouTube ecosystem:

Creators and Viewers: Creators aim to produce compelling content that resonates with viewers. They attract and retain viewers through engaging videos, consistent uploads, and building a loyal community. Creators rely on viewers for their support, including views, likes, comments, and subscriptions, which contribute to their success and growth.

Creators and Advertisers: Advertisers recognize the influence and reach of popular YouTube channels and collaborate with creators for brand partnerships. Creators may promote products or services in their videos, sponsored content, or through other advertising formats. These partnerships provide opportunities for creators to monetize their channels and generate revenue.

Viewers and Advertisers: Viewers play a crucial role in the advertising ecosystem on YouTube. They consume video content and engage with ads displayed during or around videos. Viewers' engagement, such as ad views, clicks, and conversions, is valuable to advertisers as it helps them measure the effectiveness of their campaigns and reach their target audience.

YouTube's Role: YouTube provides a comprehensive platform that facilitates content creation, distribution, and monetization. It offers tools for video uploading, editing, and analytics. YouTube's algorithms determine the visibility of videos through search results, recommendations, and trending sections, impacting the exposure and success of creators. Additionally, YouTube provides advertising options for businesses to promote their products and services, generating revenue for both YouTube and creators.

Key Terms and Concepts for YouTube Success

To navigate the YouTube ecosystem effectively, it's essential to understand key terms and concepts related to YouTube success. Let's introduce some of these:

SEO (Search Engine Optimization): SEO involves optimising video titles, descriptions, tags, and other elements to improve the visibility of videos in search results. Understanding SEO helps creators attract more viewers organically.

Engagement: Engagement refers to the interaction between viewers and video content. It includes likes, comments, shares, and subscriptions. High engagement signals viewer interest and helps videos gain visibility.

Monetization: Monetization involves earning revenue from a YouTube channel. This can be through ads, channel memberships, merchandise sales, brand partnerships, and other forms of monetization offered by YouTube.

Analytics: YouTube Analytics provides data and insights about a channel's performance, including views, watch time, audience demographics, and traffic sources. Analysing these metrics helps creators make informed decisions to optimise their content strategy.

Community Building: Building a community involves fostering a loyal and engaged audience. This includes responding to comments, engaging in conversations, and creating a sense of belonging among viewers.

Understanding these terms and concepts will enable creators to navigate the YouTube ecosystem strategically and make informed decisions to drive their success.

In Conclusion

The YouTube ecosystem is a dynamic and interconnected network where creators, viewers, advertisers, and YouTube itself collaborate to create a vibrant platform for video content. Each component plays a vital role in shaping the success and growth of creators on YouTube. By understanding the roles and interactions within this ecosystem and familiarising oneself with key terms and concepts, creators can navigate the platform effectively and maximise their chances of achieving YouTube success. In the next chapter, we'll delve into the importance of finding your niche and establishing your unique identity on YouTube.

Chapter 4:
Finding Your Niche

In this chapter, we'll embark on a journey of self-discovery to help you find your niche on YouTube. We'll explore the importance of choosing a specific niche or target audience and provide strategies for identifying your unique value proposition. Finding your niche is a crucial step towards building a successful YouTube channel, so let's dive in.

Discovering Your Passions and Interests

The first step in finding your niche is to identify your passions and interests. Ask yourself: What topics or activities do you genuinely enjoy? What makes you excited and motivated? Take some time to reflect on your hobbies, skills, knowledge, and experiences. These personal interests can serve as the foundation for your YouTube channel.

Consider the activities that bring you joy and the topics you find yourself constantly drawn to. Whether it's cooking, fashion, gaming, technology, fitness, music, or any other area, discovering your true passions will provide the fuel and enthusiasm needed to create engaging content.

THE YOUTUBE SUCCESS FORMULA: THE BLUEPRINT FOR GROWTH

The Importance of Choosing a Specific Niche or Target Audience

Once you have identified your passions, it's crucial to narrow down your focus and choose a specific niche or target audience. Here's why it's important:

Differentiation: YouTube is a crowded platform with countless creators covering a wide range of topics. By choosing a specific niche, you can stand out from the competition and establish yourself as an expert or authority in that particular area. Differentiation helps you attract a dedicated audience who is interested in your niche and more likely to engage with your content.

Audience Engagement: A specific niche allows you to connect deeply with your target audience. When you cater to a particular group of people with shared interests, you can create content that resonates with them on a personal level. This leads to higher viewer engagement, including likes, comments, shares, and ultimately, a loyal subscriber base.

Monetization Opportunities: A well-defined niche opens doors to monetization opportunities. Brands and advertisers are more likely to collaborate with creators who have a specific niche and a dedicated audience. They are looking to reach targeted demographics, and by specialising in a particular area, you position yourself as an attractive partner for sponsorships and brand deals.

Strategies for Identifying Your Unique Value Proposition

Now, let's dive into strategies for identifying your unique value proposition—the distinctive qualities that set you apart from other creators in your niche:

Self-Reflection: Look inward and assess your unique qualities, skills, experiences, and perspectives. What makes you different? What expertise or insights can you bring to your niche? Embrace your individuality and let it shine through your content.

Research Your Niche: Conduct thorough research to understand the existing content landscape within your chosen niche. Identify gaps or areas that are underserved. This research will help you find opportunities to offer something unique and valuable to your target audience.

Audience Analysis: Get to know your target audience intimately. Understand their needs, preferences, pain points, and aspirations. Engage with them through comments, surveys, or social media interactions. This deeper understanding will enable you to tailor your content to their specific interests and provide value that resonates with them.

Test and Iterate: As you start creating content, pay attention to what works and what doesn't. Analyse the performance of your videos, engagement metrics, and feedback from your audience. Use this information to refine your content strategy and continuously improve.

Embrace Your Authenticity: Be true to yourself and embrace your unique personality and style. Authenticity is a powerful asset on YouTube, as viewers appreciate genuine and relatable creators. Don't be afraid to let your true self shine through your videos.

Continual Learning and Growth: Stay curious and open to learning. As you delve into your niche, expand your knowledge, and stay up to date with the latest trends and developments. This continuous growth will allow you to bring fresh perspectives and innovative ideas to your content.

Remember, finding your niche is a process that evolves over time. It's okay to experiment, try different approaches, and refine your focus as you gain more insights and feedback from your audience.

In Conclusion

Finding your niche is a vital step in building a successful YouTube channel. By discovering your passions, choosing a specific niche, and identifying your unique value proposition, you can differentiate yourself from the competition, engage with a dedicated audience, and unlock monetization opportunities. Embrace your authenticity, conduct thorough research, and continually refine your content strategy to ensure long-term success. In the next chapter, we'll delve into the art of creating compelling content that captivates your viewers.

Chapter 5:
Creating Compelling Content

In this chapter, we'll explore the art of creating compelling content that captivates your viewers. We'll discuss the key elements of engaging and shareable videos, offer tips for planning, scripting, and filming high-quality content, and share insights on storytelling, editing, and adding value to your viewers. Let's dive in and learn how to create content that keeps your audience coming back for more.

Elements of Engaging and Shareable Content

To create compelling videos, it's important to consider the following elements:

Hooking Introductions: Grab your viewers' attention right from the start. Introduce your video with an engaging hook that piques their curiosity or evokes an emotional response. This could be a compelling question, an intriguing statement, or a captivating visual.

Clear and Concise Messages: Communicate your main message or idea clearly and concisely. Structure your content in a logical and organised manner, allowing viewers to follow along easily. Avoid rambling or going off-topic, as this can lead to viewer disengagement.

Visual Appeal: Pay attention to the visual aspects of your videos. Use high-quality cameras and equipment to ensure clear visuals. Consider lighting, framing, and composition to create aesthetically pleasing shots. Visual appeal can significantly enhance viewer engagement.

Authentic and Relatable Personality: Be yourself on camera and let your authentic personality shine through. Viewers appreciate genuine and relatable creators. Share personal stories, experiences, and anecdotes to establish a connection with your audience.

Emotional Impact: Tap into the power of emotions to create a deeper connection with your viewers. Whether it's humour, inspiration, empathy, or excitement, aim to evoke emotional responses through your content. Emotionally impactful videos are more likely to be shared and remembered.

Tips for Planning, Scripting, and Filming High-Quality Videos

To create high-quality videos, consider the following tips:

Plan Your Content: Start by outlining the main points and structure of your video. Consider the objectives, key messages, and desired outcomes. This planning phase helps ensure your content is focused, organised, and delivers value to your viewers.

Scripting: While not all videos require a script, having an outline or bullet points can help keep your thoughts organised. It also ensures you cover all the important points you want to address. However, don't be afraid to improvise and let your natural personality shine through.

Filming Techniques: Invest in a good camera and microphone to capture high-quality audio and visuals. Consider the lighting conditions and use additional lighting equipment if necessary. Experiment with different angles, camera movements, and shot compositions to add visual interest to your videos.

Audio Quality: Clear and crisp audio is essential for viewer engagement. Use a quality microphone to ensure your voice is captured accurately. Minimise background noise and echo by recording in a quiet environment.

Insights on Storytelling, Editing, and Adding Value to Viewers

To create impactful content, consider the following insights:

Storytelling: Stories have a powerful impact on viewers. Use storytelling techniques to engage your audience and create a narrative arc in your videos. Begin with a captivating introduction, develop your story with a clear structure, and conclude with a memorable ending.

Editing: Editing is where your video truly comes to life. Cut out any unnecessary footage, tighten the pacing, and add visual and audio enhancements. Use transitions, music, graphics, and effects to enhance the storytelling and engage viewers.

Adding Value: Always aim to provide value to your viewers. Educate, entertain, inspire, or solve problems through your content. Understand your audience's needs and interests, and create videos that address those needs. Adding value builds trust and loyalty with your audience.

Call to Action: Encourage viewer engagement by including a call to action at the end of your videos. Ask viewers to like, comment, share, or subscribe to your channel. This helps increase engagement and grow your audience.

Remember, creating compelling content is a continuous learning process. Analyse viewer feedback, track performance metrics, and adapt your content strategy accordingly. Experiment with different formats, styles, and topics to find what resonates best with your audience.

In Conclusion

Creating compelling content is a crucial element of YouTube success. By incorporating the elements of engaging and shareable videos, planning and scripting effectively, filming high-quality footage, and mastering storytelling and editing techniques, you can captivate your audience and keep them coming back for more. Remember to add value to your viewers and always strive to improve and evolve your content. In the next chapter, we'll dive into the world of video optimization and discuss strategies for increasing your visibility on YouTube.

Chapter 6:
Optimising Video SEO

In this chapter, we'll explore the importance of search engine optimization (SEO) on YouTube and provide strategies for optimising various elements of your videos to increase visibility and reach. We'll discuss optimising video titles, descriptions, and tags, as well as thumbnail design, video length, and engagement metrics. Let's dive in and learn how to optimise your videos for maximum impact.

The Importance of Search Engine Optimization (SEO) on YouTube

Search engine optimization plays a crucial role in making your videos discoverable on YouTube. By optimising your videos for relevant keywords and improving their visibility in search results and suggested videos, you increase the chances of reaching a larger audience. SEO helps you attract organic traffic, gain more views, and grow your subscriber base. Now, let's explore some strategies for optimising key elements of your videos.

Optimising Video Titles, Descriptions, and Tags

Video Titles: Craft compelling titles that accurately represent your video content and incorporate relevant keywords. A clear and concise title can capture viewers' attention and entice them to click on your video. However, avoid clickbait or misleading titles, as they can harm your channel's credibility.

Descriptions: Write informative and keyword-rich descriptions that provide additional context about your video. Include relevant keywords naturally, but avoid keyword stuffing. Use the description to provide a summary of your video, include timestamps for different sections, and promote any relevant links or social media accounts.

Tags: Select relevant tags that accurately describe your video's content. Use a mix of broad and specific tags to improve the chances of your video appearing in related searches. Consider using tools like YouTube's autocomplete feature or external keyword research tools to identify popular and relevant tags.

Thumbnail Design, Video Length, and Engagement Metrics

Thumbnail Design: Create visually appealing and attention-grabbing thumbnails that accurately represent your video's content. Use high-quality images or screenshots, add bold and clear text, and consider using contrasting colours to make your thumbnails stand out. Thumbnails that evoke curiosity or emotions are more likely to attract clicks.

Video Length: While video length can vary depending on the content and target audience, it's generally recommended to keep your videos concise and engaging. Avoid unnecessary filler content and aim to deliver value to viewers within a reasonable timeframe. Analyse your audience retention metrics to identify optimal video lengths for your channel.

Engagement Metrics: YouTube's algorithm considers engagement metrics like watch time, likes, comments, and shares when ranking videos. Encourage viewer engagement by asking questions, encouraging discussions in the comments, and responding to comments promptly. Engage with your audience through call-to-actions, polls, or interactive elements within your videos.

Video Transcriptions: Adding accurate transcriptions or captions to your videos can enhance their accessibility and improve SEO. Transcriptions help YouTube understand the context and content of your video, increasing the chances of it appearing in relevant search results.

Remember, optimising your videos for SEO is an ongoing process. Monitor the performance of your videos, track keyword rankings, and adjust your optimization strategies as needed. Regularly analyse YouTube Analytics to gain insights into viewer behaviour and engagement.

In Conclusion

Optimising your videos for SEO is crucial to increase their visibility and reach on YouTube. By optimising video titles, descriptions, and tags, creating visually appealing thumbnails, keeping your videos engaging and concise, and analysing engagement metrics, you can improve your chances of attracting organic traffic and growing your audience. Remember to provide value to your viewers and continuously refine your optimization strategies. In the next chapter, we'll

THE YOUTUBE SUCCESS FORMULA: THE BLUEPRINT FOR GROWTH

explore the power of collaborations and networking on YouTube.

Chapter 7:
Building an Engaged Community

In this chapter, we'll explore the significance of building a loyal subscriber base on YouTube and discuss effective techniques for engaging with viewers and fostering a strong community around your channel. We'll delve into the importance of responding to comments, collaborations with other creators, and the power of live streaming. Let's dive in and learn how to build an engaged community of loyal supporters.

The Significance of Building a Loyal Subscriber Base

Building a loyal subscriber base is essential for long-term success on YouTube. Here's why it matters:

Community Support: Loyal subscribers are your most dedicated supporters. They watch your videos, leave comments, like, and share your content. They become advocates for your channel and help spread the word, attracting more viewers and potential subscribers.

Audience Engagement: A loyal subscriber base leads to higher engagement metrics. When your community is engaged, they are more likely to watch your videos in their entirety, leave meaningful comments, and participate in discussions. This engagement not only boosts your video's performance but also creates a sense of belonging within your community.

Collaboration Opportunities: As your subscriber base grows, you have a higher chance of attracting collaboration opportunities with other creators. Brands and companies also take notice of channels with a loyal following, making it easier to secure sponsorships and partnerships.

Techniques for Engaging with Viewers and Fostering Community

To build an engaged community, consider the following techniques:

Responding to Comments: Take the time to read and respond to comments on your videos. Show genuine interest in your viewers' thoughts, questions, and feedback. Engage in meaningful conversations, provide further insights, and express gratitude for their support. This interaction creates a sense of connection and fosters a loyal community.

Community Tab and YouTube Stories: Utilise YouTube's Community Tab and YouTube Stories features to share updates, behind-the-scenes content, polls, or exclusive previews with your subscribers. Encourage them to engage by asking for their opinions, responding to polls, or sharing their own stories related to your content.

Collaborations with Other Creators: Collaborating with other creators exposes your channel to new audiences and expands your reach. Seek collaborations with creators who share a similar target audience or complementary content. Joint videos, shout-outs, or collaborative projects can be mutually beneficial and help build a sense of community between channels.

Live Streaming: Live streaming provides an interactive platform to engage directly with your subscribers in real-time.

Host live Q&A sessions, special events, or behind-the-scenes content. Respond to viewer comments and questions during the stream, making them feel involved and valued.

Community Guidelines: Establish clear community guidelines that promote positive and respectful interactions. Encourage constructive discussions while discouraging hate speech, harassment, or spam. Enforce these guidelines consistently to maintain a welcoming and inclusive community.

Tips for Effective Community Building

Here are some additional tips to enhance your community-building efforts:

Consistency: Consistently upload high-quality content to maintain the interest and engagement of your community. Establish a regular upload schedule and communicate it to your subscribers, setting expectations and keeping them excited for upcoming videos.

Subscriber Recognition: Show appreciation for your subscribers' support. Highlight and recognize loyal community members in your videos, social media posts, or live streams. This recognition makes them feel valued and encourages others to engage actively.

Engage on Social Media: Expand your community-building efforts beyond YouTube by actively engaging with your audience on social media platforms. Respond to comments, messages, and mentions, and share updates and exclusive content across multiple channels.

THE YOUTUBE SUCCESS FORMULA: THE BLUEPRINT FOR GROWTH

User-Generated Content: Encourage your community to create and submit their own content related to your channel. This could be fan art, reaction videos, or creative projects. Showcase their work in your videos or social media posts, further strengthening the sense of community.

Remember, building an engaged community takes time and effort. Be patient, authentic, and consistent in your interactions. Encourage meaningful conversations, foster a positive and inclusive environment, and adapt your community-building strategies based on your audience's preferences and feedback.

In Conclusion

Building an engaged community is a vital aspect of YouTube success. By responding to comments, fostering collaborations, utilising live streaming, and implementing effective community-building techniques, you can cultivate a loyal subscriber base and create a strong sense of community around your channel. Engaging with your audience creates a deeper connection, encourages participation, and drives long-term growth. In the next chapter, we'll explore monetization strategies and the various avenues available to generate revenue from your YouTube channel.

Chapter 8:
Monetization Strategies

In this chapter, we'll explore the various ways to monetize your YouTube channel. We'll discuss the YouTube Partner Program, ad revenue, brand partnerships, and alternative revenue streams such as merchandise and crowdfunding. Let's dive in and learn how to turn your YouTube passion into a sustainable source of income.

The YouTube Partner Program (YPP) is the primary monetization avenue for many YouTubers. To be eligible for YPP, your channel must meet certain requirements, including having at least 1,000 subscribers and 4,000 watch hours in the past 12 months. Once accepted into YPP, you can monetize your videos through ads.

Ad revenue is generated when ads are displayed before, during, or after your videos. YouTube shares a portion of the revenue with content creators based on factors like ad engagement, viewer demographics, and ad formats. Ad revenue can fluctuate based on factors such as viewer location, ad-blocker usage, and advertiser demand.

THE YOUTUBE SUCCESS FORMULA: THE BLUEPRINT FOR GROWTH

Brand partnerships offer another avenue for monetization. When you collaborate with brands, they may sponsor your videos or provide products for review. Sponsored content involves featuring or promoting a brand's product or service in your videos in exchange for compensation. It's important to disclose sponsored content transparently to maintain trust with your audience.

When pursuing brand partnerships, focus on aligning with brands that resonate with your content and target audience. Ensure that the brand's values and messaging align with your own, as authenticity is key to maintaining the trust of your viewers.

Alternative Revenue Streams: Merchandise and Crowdfunding

Beyond traditional monetization methods, there are alternative revenue streams to explore:

Merchandise: Create and sell branded merchandise related to your channel. This can include clothing, accessories, or even digital products like e-books or presets. Platforms like Teespring, Spreadshirt, or custom e-commerce websites make it easy to design, produce, and sell merchandise to your audience.

Crowdfunding: Crowdfunding platforms like Patreon, Ko-fi, or Kickstarter allow your viewers to support your channel financially. You can offer exclusive content, early access, or other perks to your supporters in exchange for their contributions. Crowdfunding provides a direct way for your loyal viewers to support you and your content.

When considering alternative revenue streams, take into account your audience's preferences and interests. Choose merchandise or crowdfunding options that align with your brand and resonate with your viewers.

Sponsored Videos and Product Placements

In addition to brand partnerships, you can explore sponsored videos and product placements. Sponsored videos involve creating content around a specific product or service in exchange for compensation. Product placements involve incorporating a brand's product organically within your videos. Both methods require transparency and clear disclosure to maintain trust with your audience.

It's crucial to select sponsorships and product placements that align with your channel's niche and values. Avoid promoting products or services that may be irrelevant or misleading to your audience, as it can erode trust and credibility.

In Conclusion

Monetizing your YouTube channel involves leveraging various strategies to generate revenue. The YouTube Partner Program and ad revenue are popular ways to monetize your videos, while brand partnerships and sponsored content offer additional opportunities. Exploring alternative revenue streams like merchandise sales and crowdfunding can also supplement your income. When pursuing monetization, prioritise authenticity, transparency, and alignment with your audience's interests. As your channel grows, continually evaluate and adapt your monetization strategies to ensure a sustainable and successful YouTube career. In the next chapter, we'll discuss the importance of analytics and data-driven decision-making for YouTube success.

Chapter 9:
YouTube Analytics and Insights

In this chapter, we'll explore the power of YouTube Analytics and how it can provide valuable data and insights to optimise your content. We'll introduce key metrics, discuss how to analyse data effectively, and offer strategies for tracking progress, identifying trends, and setting goals. Let's dive in and learn how to harness the power of YouTube Analytics to drive your channel's success.

Introducing YouTube Analytics and Key Metrics

YouTube Analytics is a powerful tool provided by YouTube that offers in-depth data and insights about your channel's performance. It provides valuable information about your audience, engagement, and video metrics. Here are some key metrics you should familiarise yourself with:

Views: The number of times your videos have been viewed. This metric helps gauge the overall reach and popularity of your content.

Watch Time: The total amount of time viewers have spent watching your videos. Watch time is a critical metric as it directly influences your channel's performance and monetization potential.

Audience Retention: This metric shows how well your videos are keeping viewers engaged. It indicates the average percentage of a video that viewers watch before dropping off. Higher audience retention indicates compelling content.

Engagement Metrics: These include metrics like likes, comments, shares, and subscribers gained. They reflect the level of audience engagement and can help identify popular videos and opportunities for improvement.

Traffic Sources: This metric shows where your viewers are coming from, such as YouTube search, suggested videos, or external sources like social media. Understanding traffic sources helps you optimise your video distribution strategies.

Analysing Data and Gaining Insights

To effectively analyse data and gain insights from YouTube Analytics, follow these strategies:

Identify Trends: Look for patterns or trends in your data. Identify videos with high audience retention, engagement, or views. Determine what makes these videos successful and apply those learnings to future content.

Audience Demographics: Use YouTube Analytics to understand your audience's demographics, including age, gender, and geographic location. This information helps tailor your content and engage with your target audience more effectively.

Refine Content Strategy: Analyse the performance of different video formats, topics, or styles. Identify content that resonates well with your audience and focus on creating more of it. Experiment with new ideas while staying true to your channel's niche.

Track Audience Behavior: Analyse audience retention and engagement metrics to understand viewer behaviour. Identify sections of your videos that experience high drop-off rates and work on improving those segments. Pay attention to comments and feedback to understand viewer preferences and adapt accordingly.

Tracking Progress, Setting Goals, and Iterating

To track your progress, set goals, and iterate based on data-driven insights, follow these strategies:

Set SMART Goals: Define specific, measurable, attainable, relevant, and time-bound (SMART) goals for your channel. For example, increasing watch time by 20% over the next three months. Set milestones and regularly evaluate progress.

Track Key Metrics: Continuously monitor your key metrics to gauge your channel's growth and performance. Set up a regular review schedule to track progress, identify trends, and make informed decisions.

Experiment and Iterate: Use data to guide your content creation strategy. Experiment with different video formats, titles, thumbnails, or topics. Measure the impact of these experiments on engagement and adjust accordingly.

Learn from Audience Feedback: Engage with your audience through comments, messages, and social media. Listen to their feedback, preferences, and suggestions. Incorporate their insights into your content strategy to strengthen the connection with your viewers.

THE YOUTUBE SUCCESS FORMULA: THE BLUEPRINT FOR GROWTH

In Conclusion

YouTube Analytics provides valuable data and insights that can help optimise your content strategy, engage with your audience, and drive channel growth. By familiarising yourself with key metrics, analysing data effectively, and setting goals based on data-driven insights, you can make informed decisions and continuously improve your channel. Embrace experimentation, adapt based on audience feedback, and iterate your content strategy to maximise your YouTube success. In the next chapter, we'll explore the importance of branding and creating a cohesive identity for your YouTube channel.

Chapter 10:
Dealing with Copyright and Legal Issues

In this chapter, we'll address copyright concerns and the importance of understanding fair use. We'll discuss how to handle content claims and disputes, and provide guidance on avoiding legal pitfalls and protecting your intellectual property. It's crucial to navigate the world of copyright and legal issues properly to ensure a successful and compliant YouTube channel. Let's explore these topics in detail.

Understanding Copyright and Fair Use

Copyright is a legal protection that grants exclusive rights to creators of original works, such as music, videos, images, and text. As a content creator on YouTube, it's essential to respect copyright laws and understand fair use. Fair use allows limited use of copyrighted material without permission for purposes such as commentary, criticism, parody, or educational use.

To navigate copyright issues effectively:

Educate Yourself: Familiarise yourself with copyright laws in your country or region. Understand what constitutes copyright infringement and how fair use applies to your content.

THE YOUTUBE SUCCESS FORMULA: THE BLUEPRINT FOR GROWTH

Create Original Content: Focus on creating original content that doesn't infringe upon the rights of others. Use your unique voice, ideas, and creativity to produce videos that stand out.

Handling Content Claims and Disputes

Content claims and disputes may arise when your videos contain copyrighted material. Here's how to handle them:

Content ID Claims: YouTube's Content ID system scans videos for copyrighted material and may result in automatic claims by copyright owners. If you receive a Content ID claim, you have several options: acknowledge the claim and let the copyright owner monetize the video, replace the copyrighted content, or dispute the claim if you believe it's in error.

Manual Claims: Copyright owners can manually claim videos that contain their copyrighted material. If you receive a manual claim, you can choose to remove or edit the copyrighted content, dispute the claim if you have the right to use the material, or reach a resolution with the copyright owner.

Disputing Claims: If you believe that your use of copyrighted material falls within fair use or you have the necessary permissions, you can dispute a claim. Provide detailed explanations and evidence supporting your fair use argument or ownership of the content.

To protect yourself from legal issues and safeguard your intellectual property:

Use Royalty-Free and Licensed Content: Utilise royalty-free music, images, and video clips from reputable sources. Alternatively, obtain proper licence for copyrighted material you intend to use legally.

Give Proper Attribution: When using third-party content with permission, provide clear and visible attribution to the original creator. This demonstrates respect for intellectual property and helps avoid potential disputes.

Seek Legal Advice: If you have concerns about copyright or legal issues, consult with a qualified attorney who specialises in intellectual property law. They can provide guidance tailored to your specific situation.

Protect Your Own Content: Take steps to protect your original content. Consider copyrighting your work, adding watermarks or logos, and monitoring for unauthorised use. YouTube provides tools like Copyright Match and the Copyright Protection Program to help protect your content.

Stay Informed: Keep up to date with copyright law changes, YouTube's policies, and best practices for avoiding copyright infringement. YouTube's Creator Academy and legal resources can provide valuable information to help you navigate the evolving landscape.

In Conclusion

Dealing with copyright and legal issues is crucial for maintaining a successful and compliant YouTube channel. Understanding copyright laws, respecting fair use, handling content claims and disputes responsibly, and protecting your intellectual property are essential steps to take. Educate yourself, use original content, seek legal advice when necessary, and stay informed about copyright-related developments. By doing so, you can protect your channel, maintain good standing, and focus on creating content that resonates with your audience. In the next chapter, we'll delve into the importance of branding and creating a cohesive identity for your YouTube channel.

Chapter 11:
Collaborations and Cross-Promotion

In this chapter, we'll explore the benefits of collaborating with other YouTubers, provide advice on finding and approaching potential collaborators, and discuss cross-promotion techniques to expand your reach and gain new subscribers. Collaborations and cross-promotion are powerful strategies that can help you grow your YouTube channel and connect with a wider audience. Let's dive in and learn how to make the most of these opportunities.

Benefits of Collaborating with Other YouTubers

Collaborating with other YouTubers offers numerous benefits for your channel:

Expanded Reach: By collaborating with someone who has a similar or larger audience, you can expose your content to a whole new group of viewers. This can lead to increased visibility, more subscribers, and enhanced growth for your channel.

Increased Engagement: Collaborations often result in higher engagement levels, as viewers from both channels are likely to be excited about the joint content. This engagement can translate into more comments, likes, shares, and overall interaction with your videos.

Cross-Promotion: Collaborations allow you to tap into each other's audiences and cross-promote your channels. This mutual support helps both creators gain exposure and potentially attract new subscribers who may become long-term viewers.

Finding and Approaching Potential Collaborators

When seeking potential collaborators, consider the following strategies:

Research and Identify Suitable Creators: Look for YouTubers who create content in a similar niche or have an audience that aligns with yours. Consider their content style, values, and overall brand to ensure compatibility.

Engage and Build Relationships: Start by engaging with the potential collaborators' content by leaving thoughtful comments, liking their videos, and sharing their work on social media. Building a genuine connection and demonstrating support can make it easier to approach them for collaboration.

Reach Out with a Personalised Proposal: When approaching a potential collaborator, be specific about your ideas and how you believe the collaboration will benefit both parties. Tailor your proposal to their content and highlight the value you can bring to the partnership.

Be Professional and Respectful: Treat the collaboration process as a professional endeavour. Clearly communicate your expectations, be responsive, and respect their creative input. Maintain open and honest communication throughout the collaboration.

To effectively cross-promote your collaborative content and expand your reach, consider these techniques:

Co-Create Unique Content: Develop content that showcases both creators' unique strengths and engages both audiences. This can include challenges, Q&A sessions, skits, or tutorials that combine your expertise and styles.

Collaborate on Promotion: Coordinate with your collaborator on the promotion of the collaboration. Both parties should share the video across their social media platforms, mention it in their newsletters or blogs, and encourage their audience to check out the joint content.

Utilise End Screens and Cards: Incorporate end screens and cards in your collaborative videos to direct viewers to your respective channels and encourage them to subscribe or watch more of your content. This provides a seamless transition for viewers to explore your channels further.

Guest Appearances and Shoutouts: Consider featuring each other as guest appearances in your videos or giving shoutouts to your collaborator in your content. This cross-exposure can generate curiosity and interest in both channels.

Collaborative Playlists: Create playlists featuring the collaborative content and promote them on your channel and social media. Encourage your audience to explore the playlist, which provides an opportunity for viewers to discover both creators' channels.

Remember, the key to successful collaborations and cross-promotion is authenticity and mutual benefit. Ensure that the collaborations align with your brand and offer value to your audience. Collaborate with creators who share similar goals and values, and aim to build long-lasting relationships that go beyond a single collaboration.

In Conclusion

Collaborating with other YouTubers and leveraging cross-promotion techniques can significantly expand your channel's reach, increase engagement, and attract new subscribers. Research and identify suitable collaborators, approach them with personalised proposals, and maintain professional and respectful communication throughout the collaboration process. Implement cross-promotion strategies to maximise exposure and create a win-win situation for both parties involved. In the next chapter, we'll delve into the importance of creating a strong community around your YouTube channel.

Chapter 12:
Growing Your YouTube Channel

Introduction:

Congratulations on your journey to building a successful YouTube channel! In this chapter, we will explore strategies and techniques to help you grow your channel, increase visibility, and attract more subscribers. Growing your YouTube channel requires a combination of smart marketing, consistency, and adaptability. Let's dive into the key strategies that will propel your channel forward.

Optimising Channel Visibility:

To increase your channel's visibility, you need to optimise your channel's appearance and make it attractive to potential subscribers. This includes creating an eye-catching channel banner and logo, writing a compelling channel description, and organising your content into playlists. Utilise relevant keywords in your channel's metadata to improve its searchability and increase the chances of appearing in search results.

Crafting Irresistible Video Titles and Thumbnails:

Video titles and thumbnails play a crucial role in grabbing viewers' attention and encouraging them to click on your videos. Create compelling titles that accurately represent your content and pique viewers' curiosity. Design visually appealing thumbnails that are clear, captivating, and reflect the essence of your video. A combination of enticing titles and eye-catching thumbnails will help increase your click-through rate and attract more viewers.

Leveraging Social Media:

Social media platforms are powerful tools for promoting your YouTube channel and reaching a wider audience. Utilise platforms like Instagram, Twitter, Facebook, and TikTok to share snippets of your videos, behind-the-scenes content, and engaging updates. Interact with your audience, collaborate with other creators, and leverage trending hashtags to amplify your reach and attract new subscribers.

Harnessing the Power of Email Marketing:

Building an email list allows you to directly communicate with your audience and promote your latest videos or special announcements. Encourage viewers to subscribe to your newsletter by offering exclusive content, behind-the-scenes insights, or access to giveaways. Regularly engage with your email subscribers and provide them with valuable content to strengthen their connection with your channel.

Collaborating with Other YouTubers:

Collaborations with other YouTubers can be a powerful way to tap into their audience and expose your channel to a wider viewer base. Look for creators in your niche or related niches with a similar subscriber count or slightly larger audience and propose collaboration ideas that provide mutual benefit. Collaborative videos can bring fresh perspectives, new viewers, and increased exposure to both channels.

Staying Consistent:

Consistency is key to growing your YouTube channel. Develop a consistent upload schedule that aligns with your audience's expectations and your content creation capacity. Regularly delivering high-quality videos will help build trust with your audience and keep them engaged. Consider creating a content calendar to plan your video topics and ensure a steady stream of content.

Adapting to Algorithm Changes:

YouTube's algorithm is constantly evolving, and staying informed about its updates is crucial for channel growth. Keep an eye on YouTube's Creator Insider channel, official blog, and creator forums to stay updated on algorithm changes and best practices. Analyse your video analytics to understand how the algorithm is responding to your content, and make adjustments to optimise for better visibility and discoverability.

Engaging with Your Audience:

Building a strong and engaged community is essential for long-term channel growth. Respond to comments, encourage discussions, and foster a sense of belonging among your viewers. Use YouTube's community tab, polls, and live streams to actively engage with your audience and make them feel valued. Encourage viewers to share their feedback, ideas, and suggestions, as this can provide valuable insights for improving your content.

Conclusion:

Growing your YouTube channel requires a combination of strategic marketing, consistent content creation, and adaptability. By optimising your channel's visibility, crafting enticing titles and thumbnails, leveraging social media and email marketing, collaborating with other creators, staying consistent, adapting to algorithm changes, and engaging with your audience, you'll be on your way to attracting more subscribers and achieving long-term success on YouTube. Embrace these strategies, be patient, and remember that building a thriving YouTube channel is a journey that requires dedication and persistence.

Keep creating, keep innovating, and watch your channel flourish!

Chapter 13:
Overcoming Challenges and Burnout

In this chapter, we'll address the common challenges faced by YouTubers and provide strategies for managing burnout and staying motivated. Building a successful YouTube channel requires perseverance, resilience, and a proactive approach to overcoming obstacles. We'll also share stories of successful creators who faced challenges and emerged stronger. Let's dive in and explore how to navigate the ups and downs of the YouTube journey.

Common Challenges Faced by YouTubers

Lack of Growth: It's common for new YouTubers to experience slow growth or a stagnant subscriber count. It can be disheartening when your hard work doesn't yield immediate results. Remember that building an audience takes time, and consistent effort is key.

Content Burnout: Consistently creating high-quality content can be physically and mentally draining. Coming up with fresh ideas, scripting, filming, and editing can take a toll on your creativity. Content burnout is a challenge many YouTubers face.

Negative Feedback and Trolls: Being in the public eye makes you susceptible to negative comments, criticism, and online trolls. Dealing with negativity can be emotionally challenging and affect your motivation and self-esteem.

Time Management: Balancing YouTube with other responsibilities, such as work, education, or family, can be demanding. Finding enough time to create content, engage with your audience, and handle administrative tasks can be a juggling act.

Strategies for Managing Burnout and Staying Motivated

Take Breaks: Allow yourself time to rest and recharge. Taking breaks from content creation can help prevent burnout and keep your creativity flowing. Use this time to explore new interests, gain inspiration, or simply relax.

Set Realistic Goals: Break down your long-term goals into smaller, achievable milestones. Celebrate your progress along the way, and don't be too hard on yourself if things don't go exactly as planned. Adjust your goals as needed.

Seek Support and Connect with Other Creators: Surround yourself with a supportive community of fellow YouTubers who understand the challenges you face. Share experiences, exchange advice, and offer each other encouragement. Online communities and local creator meetups can be great resources.

Prioritise Self-Care: Take care of your physical and mental well-being. Get enough sleep, eat nutritious meals, exercise regularly, and engage in activities that bring you joy. Prioritising self-care helps maintain your overall well-being and sustains your motivation.

Embrace Creativity and Experimentation: Keep your content fresh and exciting by embracing creativity and trying new ideas. Experiment with different formats, styles, or topics to keep both yourself and your audience engaged. Don't be afraid to take risks and think outside the box.

Develop a Consistent Routine: Establish a content creation routine that works for you. Set aside specific times for scripting, filming, editing, and engaging with your audience. Having a structured routine helps you stay organised and ensures that you dedicate enough time to each aspect of your channel.

Stories of Successful Creators Overcoming Challenges

Throughout the YouTube community, numerous creators have faced and overcome challenges on their journey to success. Their stories can inspire and motivate you during difficult times. Here are a few examples:

Grace Helbig: Grace started her YouTube career by experimenting with comedy skits and vlogs. She faced initial struggles with low views and minimal growth. However, she persisted, refined her content, and eventually gained a substantial following. Grace's story showcases the importance of perseverance and evolving as a creator.

Casey Neistat: Casey faced numerous challenges throughout his YouTube journey. From financial difficulties to personal setbacks, he encountered multiple roadblocks. However, his dedication, unique storytelling style, and consistent work ethic propelled him to become one of the most influential YouTubers. Casey's story highlights the power of resilience and embracing authenticity.

Lilly Singh: Lilly faced burnout and exhaustion while juggling her YouTube channel and other commitments. However, she recognized the importance of self-care and took a break to prioritise her mental health. Lilly's story emphasises the significance of recognizing and addressing burnout to maintain long-term success.

In Conclusion

Overcoming challenges and managing burnout is an integral part of the YouTube journey. By implementing strategies such as taking breaks, setting realistic goals, seeking support, prioritising self-care, embracing creativity, and establishing a consistent routine, you can navigate challenges and stay motivated. Remember that even successful creators faced setbacks, and their stories serve as a reminder that persistence and resilience are key to achieving your goals. In the next chapter, we'll explore the future of YouTube and discuss emerging trends and opportunities.

Chapter 14:
YouTube and Beyond

In this chapter, we'll explore opportunities for expanding beyond YouTube, discuss the role of other platforms in diversifying content distribution, and share insights on building a personal brand and pursuing additional ventures. While YouTube is a powerful platform, there are various avenues to explore to enhance your online presence and grow your influence. Let's dive in and discover the possibilities beyond YouTube.

Expanding Beyond YouTube

Social Media Platforms: Utilise social media platforms such as Instagram, Twitter, Facebook, TikTok, or LinkedIn to reach a broader audience. Each platform offers unique features and audience demographics, allowing you to connect with viewers in different ways.

Podcasting: Consider starting a podcast related to your YouTube content or exploring podcast guest opportunities. Podcasts provide an audio-focused platform to engage with your audience and attract new listeners who may not regularly consume video content.

Blogging or Vlogging: Create a blog or vlog alongside your YouTube channel to provide written or visual content that complements your videos. This allows you to reach audiences who prefer consuming content in different formats.

Live Streaming: Explore live streaming platforms such as Twitch or Facebook Live to connect with your audience in real-time. Live streams offer a more interactive and immediate way to engage with your viewers and build a dedicated community.

Diversifying Content Distribution

E-books or Digital Products: Consider creating e-books, digital guides, or educational resources related to your niche. These products can provide additional value to your audience and serve as a source of passive income.

Online Courses or Workshops: Share your expertise and knowledge by creating online courses or hosting workshops. Platforms like Udemy or Teachable allow you to monetize your knowledge and provide in-depth education to your audience.

Brand Collaborations and Sponsorships: Collaborate with brands and explore sponsorships to diversify your revenue streams. As your influence grows, brands may approach you for partnerships, or you can reach out to companies that align with your content and values.

Building a Personal Brand

Consistent Branding: Develop a strong personal brand by maintaining consistent visuals, messaging, and values across all your platforms. This helps your audience recognize and connect with your content, fostering loyalty and trust.

Authenticity and Storytelling: Share your unique story and experiences to connect with your audience on a deeper level. Authenticity resonates with viewers and helps build a genuine connection that sets you apart from others.

Engaging with Your Community: Actively engage with your audience through comments, direct messages, or live interactions. Respond to their questions, acknowledge their support, and foster a sense of community around your brand.

Pursuing Additional Ventures

Public Speaking and Events: Leverage your expertise and speaking skills by participating in industry conferences, workshops, or hosting your own events. Speaking engagements provide opportunities to share your knowledge, network, and build your personal brand.

Merchandise and Product Development: Explore the creation of merchandise, such as branded clothing, accessories, or digital products. These items can serve as additional revenue streams and allow your audience to support you in a tangible way.

Media Opportunities: Pursue media opportunities such as guest appearances on TV shows, interviews on podcasts, or collaborations with other content creators. These collaborations expand your reach and introduce you to new audiences.

THE YOUTUBE SUCCESS FORMULA: THE BLUEPRINT FOR GROWTH

In Conclusion

While YouTube is a powerful platform, there are numerous opportunities to expand your reach and influence beyond it. By exploring social media platforms, podcasting, blogging or vlogging, live streaming, and diversifying content distribution through e-books, online courses, or brand collaborations, you can extend your impact and create additional revenue streams. Remember to build a strong personal brand by maintaining consistency, authenticity, and engagement with your community. Pursue additional ventures such as public speaking, merchandise development, and media opportunities to further enhance your presence. The possibilities beyond YouTube are vast, and by exploring these avenues, you can continue to grow and thrive in the digital space. In the final chapter, we'll recap the key insights from the book and offer final thoughts on achieving success on YouTube.

Chapter 15:
Looking Ahead: The Future of YouTube

In this final chapter, we'll explore the future of YouTube and discuss emerging trends and technologies that are shaping the platform. We'll offer predictions and insights into potential developments and encourage readers to stay adaptable and embrace change. The digital landscape is constantly evolving, and it's essential to stay informed and proactive.

Let's dive in and take a glimpse into what the future holds for YouTube.

Evolving Content Formats: As technology advances, we can expect to see new and innovative content formats on YouTube. Virtual reality (VR) and augmented reality (AR) are gaining popularity, providing immersive experiences for viewers. Additionally, interactive videos, 360-degree videos, and live streaming will continue to evolve, enhancing viewer engagement and participation.

AI and Personalization: Artificial intelligence (AI) will play a significant role in shaping the future of YouTube. AI algorithms will become smarter in understanding viewers' preferences and recommending personalised content. Creators will have access to advanced analytics and insights, enabling them to tailor their content to specific audience segments.

Mobile and On-the-Go Consumption: With the increasing use of smartphones and tablets, mobile consumption of YouTube content will continue to rise. The platform will further optimise its mobile experience, offering features tailored for on-the-go viewers, such as vertical video formats and short-form content.

Diverse and Inclusive Content: The future of YouTube will prioritise diversity and inclusivity. We can expect to see a broader representation of voices, cultures, and perspectives on the platform. Creators who champion inclusivity will gain prominence, and the YouTube community will become more diverse and supportive.

Enhanced Monetization Opportunities: YouTube will continue to evolve its monetization options for creators. We can anticipate new revenue streams, such as membership subscriptions, fan funding, and direct ad partnerships. YouTube may also explore new ways to reward creators for their engagement, audience growth, and community-building efforts.

Cross-Platform Integration: YouTube will further integrate with other platforms and technologies, providing seamless cross-platform experiences. Integration with social media platforms, streaming services, and smart devices will offer enhanced accessibility and reach for both creators and viewers.

Data Privacy and Regulation: As concerns around data privacy and content regulation grow, YouTube will likely implement stricter policies and guidelines. Creators will need to stay informed about these changes and ensure compliance to maintain a positive user experience.

Embracing the Future

To thrive in the future of YouTube, it's crucial to stay adaptable and embrace change. Here are a few tips to help you navigate the evolving landscape:

Stay Informed: Keep up-to-date with industry news, trends, and emerging technologies. Follow YouTube's official announcements, attend conferences, and engage with the creator community to stay informed about the latest developments.

Experiment and Innovate: Be open to trying new content formats, technologies, and strategies. Experimentation allows you to stay ahead of the curve and discover what resonates with your audience. Embrace innovation and be willing to take calculated risks.

Focus on Value and Authenticity: As YouTube evolves, viewers will continue to seek valuable and authentic content. Stay true to your unique voice, provide value to your audience, and maintain a genuine connection. This will differentiate you from others and foster long-term engagement.

Build a Diverse Online Presence: While YouTube is a powerful platform, it's essential to diversify your online presence. Expand to other platforms, such as social media, podcasts, or blogs, to reach a broader audience and connect with viewers in different ways.

Adapt to Changes in Monetization: Keep track of YouTube's monetization options and adapt your strategies accordingly. Explore multiple revenue streams, such as brand partnerships, merchandise, or online courses, to diversify your income sources.

THE YOUTUBE SUCCESS FORMULA: THE BLUEPRINT FOR GROWTH

Nurture Community and Engagement: Community-building will continue to be crucial in the future of YouTube. Foster engagement, respond to comments, collaborate with other creators, and actively participate in your community. Building a loyal and supportive audience will be instrumental in your long-term success.

In conclusion, the future of YouTube holds exciting possibilities and opportunities for creators. By staying adaptable, embracing emerging technologies, and prioritising value and authenticity, you can thrive in the evolving digital landscape. Stay informed, experiment, and build a diverse online presence to maximise your reach and impact. Remember, the journey as a YouTube creator is an ongoing one, and by adapting to change, you can continue to grow, evolve, and succeed.

Part-2

The youtube success stories.

Liza Koshy:

Liza Koshy, a vibrant and talented content creator, has risen to fame through her unique brand of humour and relatable content on YouTube. With her infectious personality and creative videos, she has captured the hearts of millions of viewers worldwide. In this chapter, we will delve into Liza Koshy's success story, exploring her journey, the key elements that contributed to her popularity, and the impact she has had on the YouTube community.

Early Beginnings

Liza Koshy, born on March 31, 1996, in Houston, Texas, first entered the entertainment scene through Vine, a now-defunct platform for sharing short-form videos. Her short comedic clips quickly gained popularity, and she amassed a significant following on Vine before transitioning to YouTube.

YouTube Journey

In 2015, Liza Koshy created her self-titled YouTube channel and began uploading videos that showcased her natural comedic talent, charm, and ability to connect with her audience. Her content ranged from hilarious skits and parodies to vlogs and challenges. Liza's ability to inject humour into everyday situations resonated with viewers, drawing them in and keeping them engaged.

Authenticity and Relatability

One of the key factors contributing to Liza Koshy's success is her authenticity. She embraces her unique personality and isn't afraid to be vulnerable and share personal experiences with her audience. Liza's relatability stems from her ability to find humour in everyday life, making her content universally appealing.

Positive Energy and Inclusivity

Liza Koshy's positive energy is contagious. Her videos are filled with infectious laughter, uplifting messages, and a genuine desire to spread joy. She creates an inclusive environment where viewers from different backgrounds and walks of life feel welcomed and represented.

Collaborations and Connections

Liza Koshy has collaborated with numerous popular YouTubers and celebrities, including fellow content creators, musicians, and actors. These collaborations have allowed her to expand her audience and introduce her content to new viewers. By fostering connections within the YouTube community, Liza has strengthened her influence and built a supportive network of creators.

Beyond YouTube

Liza Koshy's success on YouTube has transcended the platform itself. She has gone on to host and appear in various television shows and movies, further expanding her reach and showcasing her talent to a broader audience. Her magnetic personality and comedic timing have garnered her opportunities in both traditional media and digital platforms.

Social Impact

Liza Koshy's influence extends beyond entertainment. She has used her platform to raise awareness about important social issues and promote positive change. Through her videos and collaborations, she has highlighted causes such as mental health awareness, equality, and inclusivity.

Brand Collaborations and Entrepreneurial Ventures

As her popularity grew, Liza Koshy began collaborating with brands that aligned with her values and content. These partnerships not only provided additional revenue streams but also allowed her to create unique and engaging sponsored content. Liza has also ventured into entrepreneurship, launching her own merchandise line and partnering with companies to develop branded products.

Inspiration for Aspiring Creators

Liza Koshy's success story serves as an inspiration for aspiring creators. Her journey demonstrates that authenticity, relatability, positivity, and a genuine connection with the audience can lead to immense success on YouTube. Liza's ability to adapt, grow, and diversify her content beyond the platform showcases the opportunities available to creators who are willing to explore different avenues.

In conclusion, Liza Koshy's rise to fame on YouTube is a testament to her talent, authenticity, and ability to connect with viewers. Her infectious energy, relatable content, and inclusive approach have solidified her position as one of the most beloved and influential YouTubers of her time. Liza continues to inspire and entertain millions of people worldwide, leaving a lasting impact on the YouTube community and beyond.

Markiplier:

Markiplier, the online persona of Mark Fischbach, has become one of the most recognized and influential figures on YouTube. With his engaging personality, entertaining gaming content, and philanthropic endeavours, Markiplier has captured the hearts of millions of viewers around the world. In this chapter, we will delve into Markiplier's success story, exploring his journey, the key elements that contributed to his popularity, and the impact he has had on the YouTube community.

Early Beginnings

Mark Fischbach, born on June 28, 1989, in Honolulu, Hawaii, initially pursued a career in biomedical engineering. However, his passion for gaming and creating content led him to explore the world of YouTube. In 2012, he created his YouTube channel under the name "Markiplier" and started uploading gaming videos.

Authenticity and Connection

One of the key factors that contributed to Markiplier's success is his authenticity and ability to connect with his audience. He openly shares his thoughts, emotions, and personal experiences, allowing viewers to relate to him on a deeper level. Markiplier's genuine and down-to-earth personality has fostered a strong bond between him and his viewers.

Entertaining Gaming Content

Markiplier's gaming videos are known for their energetic and enthusiastic commentary. He engages his audience through his reactions, humorous remarks, and immersive storytelling while playing a wide variety of video games. Markiplier's ability to captivate viewers with his entertaining gameplay and witty banter has made his channel a go-to destination for gaming enthusiasts.

Philanthropy and Charity Work

Beyond his gaming content, Markiplier has utilised his platform to make a positive impact on the world. He has organized numerous charity livestreams, raising millions of dollars for various causes, including mental health initiatives and organizations combating child abuse. Markiplier's philanthropic efforts have inspired his audience to come together and make a difference.

Community Engagement and Support

Markiplier values his community deeply and actively engages with his viewers. He responds to comments, participates in Q&A sessions, and interacts with fans during live streams. By fostering this sense of community and support, Markiplier has created a space where fans feel connected, valued, and empowered.

Collaborations and Partnerships

Markiplier has collaborated with other popular YouTubers, musicians, and actors, broadening his reach and introducing his content to new audiences. These collaborations have allowed him to explore different types of content and expand his creative horizons. Markiplier's willingness to collaborate and share the spotlight has helped him forge valuable relationships within the YouTube community.

Transparency and Mental Health Advocacy

In a medium often associated with curated content, Markiplier stands out for his transparency regarding his own struggles with mental health. He has openly discussed his experiences with anxiety and depression, offering support and understanding to his viewers who may be facing similar challenges. Markiplier's candidness has fostered a sense of empathy and solidarity within his community.

Beyond YouTube

Markiplier's success on YouTube has opened doors to various opportunities beyond the platform. He has ventured into voice acting, appearing in video games and animated series. Additionally, he has developed his own projects, including a graphic novel and a production company. Markiplier's willingness to explore different creative avenues demonstrates his versatility and entrepreneurial spirit.

Inspiration for Aspiring Creators

Markiplier's success story serves as an inspiration for aspiring creators. His journey showcases the power of authenticity, community engagement, and using one's platform for positive change. Markiplier's dedication to his craft, his audience, and making a difference has propelled him to the top of the YouTube landscape.

In conclusion, Markiplier's rise to fame on YouTube is a testament to his engaging personality, entertaining content, and commitment to making a positive impact. His authenticity, philanthropy, and dedication to his community have solidified his position as one of the most beloved and influential YouTubers of our time. Markiplier's continued success and contributions to the YouTube community have left an indelible mark, inspiring a new generation of creators to pursue their passions and connect with their audience in meaningful ways.

Pewdiepie:

Pewdiepie, the online alias of Felix Kjellberg, is one of the most recognizable and influential figures on YouTube. With his unique style, humour, and charismatic personality, Pewdiepie has amassed an enormous following and left a lasting impact on the YouTube community. In this chapter, we will delve into Pewdiepie's success story, exploring his journey, the key factors that contributed to his popularity, and the impact he has had on the online landscape.

Early Beginnings

Felix Kjellberg, born on October 24, 1989, in Gothenburg, Sweden, began his YouTube journey in 2010. Initially, he created videos focused on gaming commentary and walkthroughs. However, it was his distinctive comedic style and unfiltered reactions that set him apart from other content creators.

Authenticity and Unique Style

One of the main factors that propelled Pewdiepie to success is his authenticity and unique style. He fearlessly expresses his thoughts and emotions while playing video games, creating an immersive and entertaining experience for his viewers. Pewdiepie's unfiltered and genuine reactions have resonated with his audience, making them feel connected to him on a personal level.

Engaging and Interactive Content

Pewdiepie's content revolves around gaming, but it goes beyond mere gameplay. He incorporates humour, storytelling, and interactive elements that engage his viewers. Whether it's through his witty commentary, funny voices, or interactive challenges, PewDiePie creates an immersive experience that keeps his audience captivated.

Relationship with the Bro Army

PewDiePie refers to his fanbase as the "Bro Army." He has fostered a strong sense of community and connection with his viewers by encouraging engagement and interaction. PewDiePie values his audience and regularly communicates with them through comments, social media, and livestreams. This connection has created a loyal and dedicated fanbase that supports him throughout his journey.

Evolution and Adaptability

Throughout his YouTube career, PewDiePie has demonstrated his ability to adapt and evolve. He has experimented with different content styles and formats, allowing him to stay relevant and appeal to a wide range of viewers. PewDiePie's willingness to embrace change and take risks has played a significant role in his continued success.

Controversies and Resilience

PewDiePie has faced controversies throughout his career, including instances of controversial humour and accusations of inappropriate behaviour. However, he has shown resilience by taking responsibility for his mistakes, apologising when necessary, and learning from those experiences. PewDiePie's ability to navigate through challenges and emerge stronger has contributed to his longevity in the YouTube community.

Philanthropic Initiatives

Beyond his entertaining content, PewDiePie has used his platform to make a positive impact. He has participated in charitable campaigns and donated to various causes, including initiatives related to education, mental health, and environmental conservation. PewDiePie's philanthropic efforts highlight his desire to use his influence for the greater good.

Mainstream Recognition and Influence

PewDiePie's influence extends beyond YouTube. He has been recognized by mainstream media, appearing in television shows, collaborating with celebrities, and even releasing a book. PewDiePie's success has helped bridge the gap between online content creation and traditional media, further legitimising the influence of YouTubers.

Business Ventures and Entrepreneurship

PewDiePie has ventured into entrepreneurship, launching his own merchandise brand and partnering with companies for brand collaborations. He has also explored other creative endeavours, such as music and art. PewDiePie's entrepreneurial spirit and diversification of his brand showcase his ability to leverage his online success into various business ventures.

Inspiration for Aspiring Creators

PewDiePie's success story serves as an inspiration for aspiring creators. His journey demonstrates the power of staying true to oneself, embracing individuality, and building a strong connection with the audience. PewDiePie's ability to create entertaining and engaging content while staying authentic has paved the way for many aspiring YouTubers to follow their passions and find success.

In conclusion, PewDiePie's impact on the YouTube community cannot be overstated. Through his unique style, authenticity, and ability to entertain, he has amassed a massive following and influenced the online landscape. PewDiePie's journey from a gaming enthusiast to a global sensation showcases the potential of YouTube as a platform for creative expression and the power of a dedicated and engaged audience.

Dude Perfect:

Dude Perfect is a YouTube sensation known for their incredible trick shots, engaging personalities, and wholesome content. Composed of five friends - Tyler Toney, Cody Jones, Garrett Hilbert, Coby Cotton, and Cory Cotton - Dude Perfect has captured the hearts of millions with their awe-inspiring stunts, humour, and positive energy. In this chapter, we will explore the success story of Dude Perfect, examining their journey, the elements that contributed to their popularity, and the impact they have made on the YouTube community.

The Birth of Dude Perfect

The story of Dude Perfect began in 2009 when the five friends, all former high school basketball players and college roommates, decided to create a YouTube channel to showcase their incredible trick shots. They started filming themselves performing various athletic feats and shared the videos with friends and family. Little did they know that their passion project would soon turn into a global phenomenon.

Incredible Trick Shots and Engaging Content

Dude Perfect's content is centred around their amazing trick shots, which range from basketball and football to golf and ping pong. Their creativity, precision, and ability to execute seemingly impossible shots have captivated audiences worldwide. Each video is carefully crafted to keep viewers entertained, with a combination of stunning visuals, suspenseful moments, and comedic elements that make their content highly engaging and shareable.

Wholesome and Family-Friendly Appeal

One of the key factors that contributed to Dude Perfect's success is their commitment to creating wholesome and family-friendly content. They have built a reputation for producing videos that can be enjoyed by people of all ages, making them a favourite among parents and children alike. The positive and uplifting tone of their videos sets them apart in a space often associated with controversy and negativity.

Personality and Chemistry

Dude Perfect's success can also be attributed to the unique personalities and chemistry of its members. Each member brings a distinct flavour to the group dynamic, making their videos entertaining and relatable. Tyler is the energetic leader, Cody is the brains behind the operations, Garrett is the funny guy, and the Cotton twins, Coby and Cory, provide their own individual charm. This diverse mix of personalities creates a winning formula that resonates with their audience.

Record-Breaking Feats and Collaborations

Throughout their career, Dude Perfect has broken multiple Guinness World Records, further solidifying their status as masters of trick shots. Their incredible achievements, such as the longest basketball shot or the highest basketball shot, have garnered widespread attention and media coverage. Additionally, Dude Perfect has collaborated with renowned athletes, celebrities, and fellow YouTubers, broadening their reach and introducing their content to new audiences.

Building a Strong Community

Dude Perfect has always prioritised their community and actively engages with their fans. They read and respond to comments, host fan contests, and incorporate fan suggestions into their videos. By fostering this sense of community, Dude

Perfect has created a loyal and dedicated fanbase that feels connected and valued.

Brand Partnerships and Entrepreneurship

Dude Perfect's success on YouTube has opened doors to numerous brand partnerships and business ventures. They have collaborated with major brands, such as Nerf, Pringles, and Oreo, showcasing their ability to seamlessly integrate sponsored content while maintaining their authenticity. Moreover, they have expanded their brand beyond YouTube, with merchandise sales, live shows, and even a television series, solidifying their position as true entrepreneurs.

Inspiring Positivity and Philanthropy

Dude Perfect uses their platform to spread positivity and inspire others. They frequently highlight acts of kindness, showcase charitable initiatives, and encourage their viewers to make a difference in their communities. Their philanthropic efforts, such as raising funds for various causes, demonstrate their commitment to using their influence for the greater good.

Impact on the YouTube Community

Dude Perfect's impact on the YouTube community is profound. They have not only inspired countless individuals to push their limits and pursue their passions but have also set a new standard for wholesome and family-friendly content. By promoting positive values and showcasing incredible feats, Dude Perfect has left an indelible mark on the YouTube landscape.

In conclusion, Dude Perfect's journey from creating trick shot videos for fun to becoming global YouTube sensations is a testament to their talent, creativity, and commitment to their craft. Through their incredible trick shots, engaging personalities, and positive content, they have captured the hearts of millions and inspired a new generation of content creators. Dude Perfect's success story serves as a reminder that with passion, teamwork, and dedication, anything is possible in the world of YouTube.

Jenna Marbles:

Jenna Marbles, whose real name is Jenna Mourey, is a popular YouTuber known for her humorous and relatable content. With her unique personality, entertaining videos, and candid approach, she has amassed a massive following and become a prominent figure in the YouTube community. In this chapter, we will explore Jenna Marbles' success story, from her early beginnings to her impact on YouTube and the lessons we can learn from her journey.

Early Beginnings and Breakthrough

Jenna Marbles began her YouTube journey in 2010 while working various jobs and pursuing a career in writing. Her first video, titled "How to Trick People Into Thinking You're Good Looking," went viral, garnering millions of views and putting her in the spotlight. This breakthrough paved the way for her success on the platform.

Authenticity and Relatability

One of the key factors that contributed to Jenna Marbles' success is her authenticity and relatability. She is known for being unapologetically herself, sharing her thoughts, experiences, and quirky personality with her audience. Jenna Marbles' ability to connect with viewers on a personal level has allowed her to build a strong and dedicated fanbase.

Humour and Lighthearted Content

Jenna Marbles' content is characterised by her unique sense of humour and lighthearted approach. Her videos cover a wide range of topics, including everyday life, relationships, beauty, and pop culture. Whether she is trying out bizarre beauty hacks or sharing funny anecdotes, Jenna Marbles' comedic timing and wit make her content highly entertaining and enjoyable to watch.

Engaging with the Audience

Jenna Marbles values her audience and actively engages with them. She reads and responds to comments, incorporates fan suggestions into her videos, and even involves her pets in her content. By fostering this sense of interaction and community, she has created a loyal and supportive fanbase that feels connected to her on a personal level.

Evolution and Adaptability

Throughout her YouTube career, Jenna Marbles has shown a willingness to evolve and adapt to the changing landscape. She has experimented with different video formats, styles, and topics, allowing her content to stay fresh and relevant. Jenna Marbles' ability to stay true to herself while embracing new ideas has contributed to her longevity and continued success.

Addressing Controversies and Growth

Like many public figures, Jenna Marbles has faced controversies throughout her career. She has taken responsibility for her past actions, apologised when necessary, and shown growth and maturity in addressing her mistakes. Jenna Marbles' ability to learn from her experiences and take steps towards self-improvement has garnered respect from her audience.

Empowering and Inspiring Others

Jenna Marbles has used her platform to empower and inspire others. She has openly discussed personal struggles, body image issues, and mental health, creating a safe space for her viewers to relate and find comfort. By sharing her own journey, Jenna Marbles has encouraged others to embrace their uniqueness and overcome obstacles.

Impact on YouTube and Media

Jenna Marbles' impact extends beyond YouTube. She has been recognized by mainstream media and has made appearances on television shows and podcasts. Her success has showcased the influence and reach of YouTubers, bridging the gap between online content creation and traditional media.

Legacy and Lessons Learned

Jenna Marbles' success story teaches us several valuable lessons. First, being authentic and true to oneself is crucial. By embracing her unique personality and staying genuine, she has attracted a loyal following. Second, engaging with your audience and building a community fosters a stronger connection and loyalty. Finally, Jenna Marbles' journey reminds us that growth, learning, and self-improvement are essential aspects of success.

In conclusion, Jenna Marbles' rise to fame on YouTube is a testament to her authenticity, humour, and relatability. With her entertaining and engaging content, she has captured the hearts of millions and left a lasting impact on the YouTube community. Jenna Marbles' success story encourages us to embrace our true selves, connect with our audience, and continuously evolve as we pursue our passions.

Conclusion

In the digital age, YouTube has revolutionised the way we consume and engage with content. It has created a platform where anyone with a camera and a story to tell can find success and reach a global audience. Throughout this book, we have explored the world of YouTube success, delving into the journeys of influential YouTubers and uncovering the strategies and principles that have propelled them to stardom.

From the early beginnings of YouTube to its current status as a cultural phenomenon, we have witnessed the power of this platform to shape careers, connect communities, and inspire millions. We have seen how individuals with a passion for creativity, entertainment, education, and more have leveraged YouTube to build their personal brands, create compelling content, and engage with audiences in unprecedented ways.

The success stories of Liza Koshy, Markiplier, PewDiePie, Dude Perfect, and Jenna Marbles have demonstrated that there is no one path to YouTube success. Each of these individuals has carved their own unique niche, harnessing their talents, authenticity, and perseverance to stand out in a crowded digital landscape.

Through their journeys, we have learned valuable lessons. We have discovered the importance of finding our own voice, embracing our passions, and connecting with our audience on a personal level. We have witnessed the power of consistency, hard work, and adaptability in achieving long-term success. We have recognized the significance of community building, engagement, and collaboration in fostering a loyal fanbase and expanding our reach.

Moreover, we have explored the practical aspects of YouTube success, such as understanding the YouTube ecosystem, creating compelling content, optimising video SEO, building an engaged community, monetization strategies, analysing YouTube analytics, and navigating legal issues. We have equipped ourselves with the tools and knowledge to navigate the ever-evolving YouTube landscape and make informed decisions as content creators.

However, beyond the technicalities and strategies, the heart of YouTube success lies in authenticity, passion, and connection. It is about sharing our stories, inspiring others, and making a positive impact. YouTube has provided a platform for diverse voices to be heard, for communities to form, and for dreams to be realised.

As we conclude this book, it is important to acknowledge that the landscape of YouTube is constantly evolving. New trends, technologies, and challenges will continue to shape the platform. It is essential for aspiring YouTubers to stay adaptable, embrace change, and continually learn and grow. Success on YouTube requires perseverance, resilience, and a willingness to evolve with the ever-changing digital landscape.

Whether you are a content creator, an aspiring YouTuber, or simply a curious reader, this book has provided insights, inspiration, and practical guidance to navigate the exciting world of YouTube success. The stories and lessons shared by successful YouTubers have illuminated the possibilities and potential that this platform holds.

As you embark on your own YouTube journey, remember to stay true to yourself, embrace your unique voice, and create content that resonates with your audience. Embrace the power of community and collaboration, and never underestimate the impact you can make through your creativity and passion.

YouTube success is not guaranteed overnight, but with dedication, persistence, and a genuine connection with your audience, you have the opportunity to create a meaningful and impactful presence in the digital world. So go forth, tell your story, and let your YouTube success story unfold. The world is waiting to hear from you.

Good luck on your YouTube journey, and may your passion, creativity, and authenticity shine bright on this incredible platform called YouTube.

Bonus tips for new youtubers

Certainly! Here are some bonus tips for new YouTubers:

Be consistent: Consistency is key on YouTube. Try to establish a regular upload schedule and stick to it. This helps build anticipation among your audience and keeps them engaged with your content.

Focus on quality: While consistency is important, don't sacrifice quality for quantity. Take the time to create well-produced and engaging videos that resonate with your target audience. Invest in good equipment, learn editing techniques, and continuously improve your skills.

Find your niche: Discover your unique value proposition and carve out a niche for yourself on YouTube. Identify your passions, strengths, and areas of expertise. This will help you stand out from the crowd and attract a dedicated audience.

Engage with your audience: Actively engage with your viewers by responding to comments, asking for feedback, and encouraging them to participate in discussions. Building a strong relationship with your audience creates a sense of community and loyalty.

Collaborate with others: Collaborations with other YouTubers can be a powerful way to expand your reach and gain new subscribers. Look for creators within your niche or those whose content complements yours. Collaborative videos not only expose you to new audiences but also provide a fresh perspective for your existing subscribers.

Utilise social media: Leverage the power of social media to promote your YouTube channel and connect with your audience. Create accounts on platforms like Instagram, Twitter, and Facebook to share behind-the-scenes content, teasers, and updates. Engage with your followers and use relevant hashtags to reach a wider audience.

Optimise your titles, tags, and descriptions: Use keywords strategically in your video titles, tags, and descriptions to improve your visibility in YouTube search results. Research popular and relevant keywords related to your content and incorporate them thoughtfully.

Learn from analytics: Pay attention to YouTube Analytics to gain insights into your audience demographics, watch time, and viewer behaviour. This data can help you understand which videos are performing well, identify trends, and make informed decisions about your content strategy.

Be patient and persistent: Building a successful YouTube channel takes time and effort. Don't get discouraged by slow growth or initial setbacks. Stay persistent, keep improving, and learn from each experience. Success on YouTube is a journey, and with dedication and perseverance, you can achieve your goals.

Enjoy the process: Lastly, remember to have fun and enjoy the process of creating content. YouTube is a platform for self-expression and creativity. Embrace your passion, stay true to yourself, and let your personality shine through. When you genuinely enjoy what you do, it will reflect in your content and resonate with your audience.

Best of luck on your YouTube journey!

Apology note

Dear Reader,

I would like to take a moment to extend my sincere apologies for any shortcomings or disappointments you may have encountered while reading this book. It is with humility that I acknowledge that no book can be perfect, and there may have been aspects that did not meet your expectations or provide the level of depth you were seeking.

As an AI language model, my purpose is to assist and provide information to the best of my abilities. While I strive to offer comprehensive and accurate content, I recognize that my responses are generated based on patterns and information available up until September 2021. This means that some information may be outdated or incomplete, and I apologise for any inconvenience caused by this limitation.

Furthermore, I understand that simplicity of language is important in making content accessible and engaging. However, I acknowledge that there may be instances where the simplification may have oversimplified certain topics or failed to fully capture their complexity. I apologise if this has led to a lack of depth or understanding on certain subjects.

My goal is to assist and support you in your pursuit of knowledge and understanding, and I regret any instances where I may have fallen short of your expectations. Your feedback and experience are invaluable in helping me improve and provide better assistance in the future.

If there are specific areas or topics within the book where you feel more clarity or depth is needed, I encourage you to reach out and share your concerns. Your feedback will enable me to address those areas more effectively and ensure a better experience for future readers.

Once again, please accept my sincerest apologies for any shortcomings or frustrations you may have experienced while reading this book. Your interest and engagement are greatly appreciated, and I am committed to continuously improving and providing the best possible assistance to readers like you.

Thank you for your understanding, and I hope that despite any shortcomings, this book has still provided you with valuable insights and inspiration for your journey into the world of YouTube success.

Thanks:

Dear Readers,

As we come to the end of this book, I would like to take a moment to express my heartfelt gratitude and extend a warm thank you to each and every one of you. Thank you for choosing to embark on this journey into the world of YouTube success with me. Your time, interest, and engagement are deeply appreciated.

Writing this book has been a labour of love, and it would not have been possible without your support and encouragement. Your dedication to expanding your knowledge, honing your skills, and seeking inspiration is what fuels the passion behind sharing these stories and insights.

Thank you for your patience as we explored the intricacies of YouTube, its success stories, strategies, and challenges. It is my hope that this book has provided you with valuable information, practical guidance, and inspiration for your own YouTube journey.

Each and every reader brings a unique perspective, and your engagement with the content makes this book come alive. Your questions, feedback, and interactions have enriched the experience and helped create a more vibrant and dynamic exploration of YouTube success.

I am truly grateful for the opportunity to be a part of your learning and growth. Your thirst for knowledge, curiosity, and commitment to self-improvement are inspiring. I hope that this book has empowered you to pursue your dreams, embrace your uniqueness, and make a positive impact through the powerful medium of YouTube.

Remember, success on YouTube is not just about numbers and fame. It is about connecting with others, sharing your voice, and leaving a lasting impression. I encourage you to stay true to yourself, explore your passions, and create content that resonates with your audience. Your authenticity and dedication will shine through and attract those who appreciate and value your unique perspective.

Once again, thank you for joining me on this journey. Your presence and engagement have made this experience all the more fulfilling. I am immensely grateful for your readership and for allowing me to be a part of your YouTube aspirations.

I wish you all the best on your YouTube journey. May your creativity continue to flourish, your voice be heard, and your impact be felt. Remember, every great YouTuber started somewhere, and with determination and perseverance, you too can achieve your goals.

Thank you, from the bottom of my heart, for reading this book and for being a part of this incredible community of learners and creators.

With heartfelt gratitude.

Acknowledgments:

I would like to express my deepest gratitude to all those who have supported me throughout the creation of this book.

First and foremost, I would like to thank my family and friends for their unwavering encouragement and belief in my abilities. Your constant support and understanding have been instrumental in this journey, and I am truly grateful for your presence in my life.

A special thank you goes to the YouTube community, the creators who inspire and motivate me every day. Your dedication to your craft and willingness to share your knowledge and experiences have been invaluable in shaping the content of this book.

I am also indebted to the team at YouTube and the countless experts in the field who have contributed their insights and expertise. Your dedication to helping creators succeed and your commitment to fostering a vibrant and inclusive community is truly commendable.

To my editor and the publishing team, thank you for your guidance, patience, and tireless efforts in shaping this book into its final form. Your expertise and attention to detail have been invaluable, and I am grateful for the opportunity to work with such a talented group of individuals.

I would like to extend my appreciation to the readers and supporters of my YouTube channel and online community. Your feedback, comments, and engagement have been a constant source of inspiration and have fueled my passion for creating content that resonates with you.

Lastly, I want to acknowledge all the YouTubers, both big and small, who have paved the way for aspiring creators like myself. Your dedication, hard work, and success stories have served as a beacon of hope and a reminder that with perseverance, anything is possible.

To everyone who has played a part in this book, whether big or small, I am truly grateful for your contribution. Your belief in my vision and your support throughout this process have been invaluable. This book would not have been possible without each and every one of you.

Thank you from the bottom of my heart.

Alex Brightman

Don't miss out!

Visit the website below and you can sign up to receive emails whenever Alex Brightman publishes a new book. There's no charge and no obligation.

https://books2read.com/r/B-A-XEXX-HHHJC

BOOKS 2 READ

Connecting independent readers to independent writers.

Did you love *The Youtube Success Formula: The Blueprint For Growth*? Then you should read *Affiliate Marketing: The Ultimate Guide to Building a Profitable Online Business*[1] by Alex Brightman!

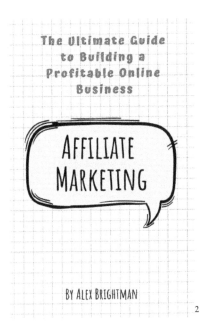

The Ultimate Guide to Building a Profitable Online Business

AFFILIATE MARKETING

BY ALEX BRIGHTMAN

2

Looking to start or grow your affiliate marketing business?

Look no further than "Affiliate Marketing" by Alex Brightman. This comprehensive guide covers everything you need to know to succeed in affiliate marketing, from building your website and creating high-quality content to leveraging social media and paid advertising. Learn how to build relationships with your audience and affiliates, track your

1. https://books2read.com/u/3nDgYK

2. https://books2read.com/u/3nDgYK

performance, overcome common challenges, and prepare for the future of affiliate marketing. Packed with real-life case studies and success stories, "Affiliate Marketing" is a must-read for anyone looking to tap into the power of affiliate marketing. Get your copy today and start building your affiliate empire!

Also by Alex Brightman

Ingram Content Group UK Ltd.
Milton Keynes UK
UKHW010726070623
423023UK00001B/26